Acknowledgements

Dear Friends & Family,

I want to thank you all for your contributions towards making this possible. Writing has always been a passion of mines for the longest and I can truly say I have progressed. Some of the errors are intentional to show my progress from when I first started until now. These poems reflect past memories and present memories and obstacles I encountered. I must admit, poetry has made my life a little bit easier. I want to thank my friends for supporting me throughout my journey and being the stepping stones I need to proceed on. Once again, thank you everyone for playing an important role in my life.

Death Row

(Apr. 27, 2011)
I fell for you, and still haven't bounced back
You walked right pass as if i was off track
You lead me down the road less traveled
having second thoughts along the way
Scared what was ahead, what the future would display?
My heart spoke loud but i couldn't quite understand
Looking at this dead end road explained this wasn't the intended plan
You were the enemy, you allowed yourself to fall in the devil's pit
Surrounded by accusers of your fate, like Oedipus
But i took on the journey despite how vigorous
I treaded through, blind-folded
allowing others to mold me
You ran right into her & she appeared the one
I put aside all insecurities, became defenseless;
dumb
The crazy things we do for love
It's scary we are so willing to lose it all;
empty
Sacrificing for the one hoping to complete many
The finger is always pointed at the corrupter
But we cannot blame the ones who simple
has not learn to love themselves first
We allow ourselves to walk down the path of love
Not quite understanding it is not the same as it was before
Each time we are hurt, it handicaps us from growing
what we encountered before
We commit our own crime
Death- Row

Lost Chronicles
(Oct. 4, 2011)

She always was like, "find the love within yourself"
I told her it's kind of hard especially when she was all i had left
She was there with me even to see the sun rise up
Our love was like the night, it was still young
Never thought this moment would ever come, young
birds in love, sprung
Even after we went our separate ways, we seemed to cross paths
We still went out and caught up and shared a couple of laughs
It was after then everything changed, Relations cut off like a bad connection
I remember like it was no other day I was crossing the street like every morning
Felt like something was about to happen, but dismissed it
I got a surprise call from my old friend , said she was in town
So i suddenly hopped in the car, excited to see her
Not knowing in less than a minute everything is about to change;
I looked at the coffee shop as I passed it, thinking about the memories that will always
remain
Then, bang, one. two.. three...
Got out the car and that is all I could remember, all I saw on the ground was the
friendship bracelet I gave her
this past December
See the crazy thing is that I ended more than her life; I ended the life of someone who I
was going to
ask to be my wife

My version of Marvin's room
(June 22, 2011)

Been a couple of years, since I last heard from you
You sent me a random text, saying shorty what it do
Yu knew I loved you like there was no future; I gave my heart like there was no use
You chose her over me now you try to ease back in my life
The scars from the past were stretch marks that reminded me of the sorrow at night
As hard as it was to move on, I struggled to push forward
Because all you was a hindrance & a played out recorder
Now I'm sitting around, happy as ever, because I met someone who
Can treat me way better
Was she really worth your newfound love, &my tragic heartbreak
When you chose to leave me for my best friend, I chose to leap off the deep-end
Looking, Searching for a fast love, to accompany my hurt & misery
That I could not simply handle
They say "everything happens for a reason," & the reason you hurt me was so
I can find someone worth believing in
It's funny how you text me saying you miss the times we had
Telling me how you're reading letters from when we was together
And im looking at the text barely want to text back
Because me caring is what I lack
Glad I left you, you was another useless letter
With no writing on the paper
Woulda said you can do better
But since im gladly taken by the best you can't do better

A tale of many
(June 17, 2011)
She was the little girl I knew, from around the way
She lived next door & had traffic of men coming in & out of the house everyday
Every Sunday you couldn't miss her on the front bench at church
Every Thursday night in the club, you would see a random man hand up her skirt
She was the pastor's daughter, and every man's fantasy
In every beauty shop, her name was mentioned in gossip, & was called Loosey Lucy
But behind every person face, is a story awaiting to be told
While many ladies were riding in fancy whips, she was riding every man's dick
It is funny how the Pastor's wife was the one insulting her daughter with vulgar language
While the pastor was the one who was financing Loosey Lucy sexual cravings.
Now you see when Lucy was thirteen, her father, now the Pastor of his own church
Laid on top of his daughter because having sex with his own wife just would not work
Mom ignored the spottings in Lucy's underwear, & chose to ignore the screams from the room
Now Loosey Lucy is the mother of two
Now this story has no happy ending, this is no Disney movie
This Alice lost herself in a wonderland, and was found dead
in the final man's bed, her dad.

Love you from a distance
Deep inside my heart
laid sorrow & fear
of letting anyone dare enter or come in
The thought of losing you
changed my state of mind
the thought of wanting you
Was to much to bear inside
Time elapsed, but for you, my love remained
Torture & abuse of the past
gave my Heart a strain

But you was too deep in yourself,
your pride, to realize
i was in love with you not for no explained reason
but far more deeper than the depth of the Mediterranean sea

The simple three words that people whisper to the ones they love, are quiet lies
that put our hearts in vain
For we are only victims of Love's game
We fight for the ones we love, and result with pain, the love we have lost
never to be regained
The saying "If it's meant to be, they will return back
You proved it true, but it seems so hard to believe that
Im scared of fighting, im scared to even try
because if i lost you once, i feel all emotions will be pushed aside

I wanna replace those lames who knew not of love
I wanna take the pain, & place it under our feet
With you & me anything is possible, Believe

As you can tell im torn between love & hate
The addicting love drug makes it impossible for my heart to escape
But in the end everyone has a lesson to learn,& i learned mines
To remember love has no heart, nor eyes

So imma take my chances and cut some loose ends
To avoid walking down the path of hurt
& only Love From a Distance

Moment in Time *(Dec. 4, 2010)*
When they say nothing lasts forever,, i say my love will always will
The moments we cherish so dear, the pain that burdens us that still lives
within our hearts, but we push on because we only progress when we can truly say we have changed from the start
But imagine if we could stop time,, the times we shared with the ones we love,,,
the ones who meant the most, imagine if time stopped and the only thing that mattered was us
There was a moment in time when everything mattered, now our hearts lay like glass, shattered
iif only we focused on what we had, not wat was to come
the love that resembled happiness,,, when we conquered together
But ii have to remind myself that was the past,,,an have to realize that nothing lasts...
that there was such a thing as love, but it disappeared as it was quicksand,,,
but now yew deny it all, the feeling you felt as ii came around, the quicken pace of your heart,,
the moments we were like the stars,,,we shined
iif only the hands of time could rewind, that time you cared,,, that moment in time

Suffering Love's Pain *(July 24, 2010)*
Suffering Love's pain
of not knowing what 2morrow holds
not understanding life's game
as we struggle to break free from its chokehold
no limits no boundaries
its all explicit
forget tryin 2 pursue dreams
and set urself out an live it
leaving behind the past
cuz the future holds greater treasure
makin our way thru life
strugglin with undeniable pressure
set for the best
live for today
for u hav not seen the worse yet
until u suffered life's pain

Holder of my Heart *(July 1, 2010)*
my heart was lost at sea and a stranger came along an found it. THEY treasured it as their own an loved it as if it was my body. When my heart was shattered by past relationships, you picked up the broken pieces a mended it with your superficial love. i took a chance with yew an had to learn how to trust, but it was so hard when I never knew what was true love. The world will never understand what held us together but right now i don't care cause it feels to good. .your loving is so sweet like the kisses I can never get enough of. .your touch is the key that unlocks my soul, your everlasting love that never will get old, our romance that many others envy, our love that holds together our hearts, the feeling of your body within me, the sexual attractions that brought us together from the start. You are truly the key that help me unlock doors to my dreams an desires. you have truly shown you are worthy of the part, as my lover, my friend, the holder of my heart

11/ 16 Random
Wet kisses across my face, smell of sex floating through the room licking my lips savoring her taste. The adrenaline rush of our pussies thumping..thump. Thump I slide underneath her, taking in the beautiful sight her titties swaying left to right, feeling her with my hands as they walk around her insides She holds back, I pull her towards me, any moment a explosion awaits at my fingertips as they tease the opening of life. I gave her life , sucked on her neck, bit on her inner thighs, fucked her mind
She screams, "Fuck Me" I spread her set of pussy lips, kissed them and slid my tongue in between, she buried her head in the pillows, I buried my face in her ocean, dived in making waves, as she begged for more, I grabbed my pussy & moaned in ecstasy

Nov.29.11

BEFORE THE SUN SETS//

BEFORE THE SUN SETS, I WANT TO TELL YOU A SECRET

I WANT TO LET YOU KNOW THAT I HAD RAINY DAYS THAT WIPED ALL
EXISTENCE OF HOPE

I TRAVELED ALONE ON MANY ROADS, BUT THEY ALL WERE JUST DEAD ENDS

I TOOK A DETOUR ON THIS ROAD CALLED RISKS; I TOOK THAT ROAD AND IT
SOMEHOW LED TO YOU

BEFORE THE SUN SETS, I WANT YOU TO KNOW YOU WAS THE LITTLE BIT OF
SUNSHINE THAT

PEAKED THROUGH

BEFORE MY LIFE DECIDES TO TAKE A TURN FOR THE WORSE, I WANT YOU TO
KNOW

THE REASON I SMILE IS ALL BECAUSE OF YOU

RISKS LED TO CHANCES ; I WAS SCARED, BUT WILLING TO TAKE

BEFORE THE SUN SETS, I WANT YOU TO KNOW YOU GAVE ME A NEW FACE

TO MY HEART

YOU GAVE MY HEART A REASON TO THROB FOR THE ABSENCE OF A HUMAN
AGAIN

BEFORE THE SUN SETS, AND WE GO OUR SEPARATE WAYS

I WANT YOU TO KNOW,BECAUSE OF YOU I WILL NEVER FORGET HOW TO LOVE

Nov.28.11

NEEDS NO TITLE//

I WALKED IN THE ROOM, FULL OF AWKWARD SILENCE

HELD HOSTAGE OF MY MIND, CHAINED BY INDESCRIBABLE NONSENSE

LETTING THE BEST OF MY INSECURITIES WRESTLE WITH MYSELF

THEY SAY LIFE IS ONLY A TEST OF TIME, THAT NEVER REWINDS

BUT LEAVES SKID MARKS OF OUR PAST, A TRACE OF LIES

TO BURDEN US TO THE POINT OF NO RETURN, WE SEE THE SIGNS

BUT CONTINUE TO TAKE A WRONG TURN

DEAD END..THE END OF A NEW BEGINNING

I WISH THAT SIDE OF ME WOULD DIE, AND REBIRTH A WHOLE NEW BEING

A ACHIEVER, WHO BELIEVES IN HERSELF AND FINDS SOMEONE WORTH LOVING

Nov.27.11
SORRY, I'M JUST THAT COMPLICATED...//

I DON'T WANT ANYONE TO LOVE ME FOR ME, BUT FOR THE PERSON I'M DESTINED TO BE
DON'T JUDGE ME BY MY APPEARANCE, BUT AKNOWLEDGE MY DIFFERENCE
I AM NOT WHAT I SAY, BUT HOW I LET MY ACTIONS SPEAK
FOR BEAUTY LIES WITHIN ONE'S SOUL, CUT-THROAT DEEP
I WANT TO BECOME JIG-SAW PUZZLES, THAT BAFFLES THE MIND
SO IF THEY CAN SOLVE & CHALLENGE ME , THEY TRULY DESERVE TO BE MINE

Nov.27.11
NEVER LET GO//

WHY WON'T YOU JUST TELL ME YOU HATE ME, AND SAY HOW UGLY I AM
OR SAY HOW I'LL NEVER BECOME ONE OF YOUR FANTASIES
WHY WON'T YOU TELL ME , HOW MUCH YOU HATE WHEN I SMILE
OR HOW HAPPY YOU GET WHEN I'M DEPRESSED AND DOWN
WHY WON'T YOU TELL ME YOU RE CHEATING BECAUSE I'M TOO KIND
OR HOW I WILL NEVER AMOUNT TO ALL THE BAD ASS BITCHES YOU SEE ON MTV LIVE
WHY WON'T YOU TELL ME THAT IM TOO INSECURE, CAPRICIOUS, AND UNSURE
AND WHY YOU NEVER WANT TO TOUCH ME BECAUSE I'M PURE
WHY WONT YOU BE SO KIND AND BE HONEST ABOUT HOW YOU FEEL
THAN, SNEAK BEHIND MY BACK AND CHEAT,
RAPE MY HEART & BURN IT IN A SCORCHING FIELD

Nov.24.11
IT'S CRAZY…//

HOW I EMBRACE THE MOST PECULIAR THINGS IN LIFE AND BECOME AMUSED

I LOOK IN THE MIRROR AND SEE PAIN, HURT AND ABUSE

BUT I LOOK BEHIND ME, IN THE PAST TO WHERE I AM NOW

DEEP, DEEP INSIDE MY HEART CRIES ALOUD

ONLY I CAN HEAR IT, AND KNOW WHAT IT SUFFERS

BUT I CAN STILL PUT ASIDE MY ISSUES FOR ANOTHER

PERSON

AND TELL THEM THEY ARE STRONG, ONE OF A KIND AND WILL BE THE KEY TO THEIR SUCCESS

IT'S CRAZY BECAUSE WHEN I SEE THEM SMILE, IM BETTER YET,

AGAIN

SOMETIMES..//

I WISH I WAS A STAR, IN THE MIDNIGHT SKIES

SO WHERE EVER YOU MAY GO, I LL BE RIGHT

BY YOUR SIDE, ILL LEAD THE WAY TO THE CENTER OF YOUR HEART

AND IF YOU LET ME, I WONT LET YOU FORGET ME, BUT IF YOU DO

DON'T NEGLECT ME

WHEN YOU CRY LATE AT NIGHT, I WILL FALL OUT OF THE SKY TO CATCH THOSE TEARS

FOR WHEN I AM NOT NEAR, ILL ONLY BE A TEAR-DROP AWAY

SOMETIMES I WANT TO BE FAR AWAY FROM YOU , JUST SO I'LL KNOW HOW IT FEELS

THE URGE OF WANTING SOMEONE SO MUCH

SO WHEN WE FINALLY SEE ONE ANOTHER, YOU'LL BECOME STAR-STRUCK

Nov.23.11
MOMENTARY GOODBYES//

IT WAS THE HARDEST, BUT BITTERSWEET

BECAUSE I KNEW WHEN SHE LEFT, I WOULD LONG FOR HER ONCE AGAIN

THOUGH I KNEW THIS GOODBYE WASN'T FOR LONG, BUT I LACK PATIENCE

CRAZY I MISS HER ALREADY, AND IT HASN'T EVEN BEEN A HOUR, BUT MY HEART REACHES

OUT AS IF I HAVEN'T SEEN HER IN AWHILE

I MISS THOSE EYES, THAT WALKED INTO MY SOUL AND UNVEILED MY HEART , THAT SMILE

THAT WAS THE FUEL TO MY FIRE

THOSE HANDS THAT LEAVES YOU FEIGNING FOR HER TOUCH

BUT I KNEW DEEP DOWN INSIDE, THERE WAS NO NEED FOR MY HEART TO CRY

SO I ACCEPTED WHAT IS LAID AHEAD OF ME, FOR IT'S ONLY A MOMENTARY GOODBYE

Nov.22.11
RANDOM POETRY OF MINES//

SHE STEPPED OUTSIDE AND WALKED INTO A NEW WORLD. STANDING ON A BALCONY OF HOPES; HOPING THAT IT LL SUPPORT HER THROUGH IT ALL. LEAVING BEHIND THE PAST, HOPING TO FIND A NEW LIFE TO DISCOVER. SOMETIMES IT TAKES ONE F'KD UP LIFE FOR YOU TO SEE THINGS CLEARER. ONCE YOU PEEL BACK A WOMAN'S HURT AND PAIN, DOESN'T SHE SEEM SO BEAUTIFUL? SHE JUST TRYING TO SURVIVE, WORKING PAST HER BURDENS, TRYING TO LOOK PAST THOSE TEARS OF HERS AND REALIZE SHE HAS SOMETHING TO LIVE FOR.. HER WORTH

Nov.10.11
RANDOM POETRY //

WHEN YOU GIVE YOUR HEART, YOU ARE LEFT WITH THE REMAINS
WHY PLAY ALONG WITH FOOLISH PEOPLE, WHEN THEY ARE ALL THE SAME
I WALK AROUND WITH A "S" ON MY CHEST, I AM THE REAL HERO
I NEED NO ONE IN MY LIFE WHO IS NOT STRIVING FOR THE BEST, ZEROS
WE DEPEND ON BEING LOVED BY OTHERS, WHO PROMISE YOU THE WORLD
ALL THE WAY THROUGH, WHY WAIT TO BE SAVED WHEN THE TRUE
SUPERHERO IS YOU....

Sept. 21.11
(INSERT YOUR OWN INTERPRETATION)//

I FEEL SO FAR GONE AS IF THERE IS NO TURNING BACK

IM MOVING ALONG AS IF IM PULLING MORE THAN MY PROBLEMS

BUT THE BURDENS OF WHAT EVERYONE ELSE CARRIES OR WHAT I LACK

I GUESS ITS MY TIME TO DIG DEEP WITHIN AND FIND THAT TREASURE THAT

EVERYONE ELSE SEES

BUT MAYBE I GOT SO BLINDED BY THE FAÇADE OF POPULARITY

IM ALMOST THERE I CAN TASTE IT, IF I KNEW THIS IS WHAT WAS TO COME

I WOULD HAVE BEEN GAVE UP AND LEFT WHAT'S IN THE PAST; AS DONE

I GO THROUGH EVERYDAY THINKING THIS IS WHAT IM DESTINED TO BE

TO FIND ME THROUGH WHAT IS NOT PLAIN TO SEE TO THE NAKED EYE

BUT TO THE WORLD THEY ONLY SEE WHAT THEY WANT ME TO BE; THE RULES THEY WANT

ME TO ABIDE BY

DO THIS; CHANGE FOR ME, YOU CANT DO THIS OR THAT

MY LIFE FEELS AS IF IM A RUBIX CUBE IN TRANSFORMATION

BUT THE ONLY THING IS IM NOT CONTROLLING MY OWN LIFE

THRIVING OFF OF ONLY THE INFATUATION OF THE FAST LIFE

BREEZING BY AS IF THE WIND IS BENEATH MY WINGS; BUT SOMEHOW IM FLYING OFF OF DREAMS

SLEEPING ON THESE HATERS CAUSE THEY CANT TAKE ME WHEN IM AWAKE ; TIME TO HOLD THE CLOCK IN MY HANDS;

AND LET THE PEOPLE REALIZE I AM ME, AND ONLY I CAN CHANGE ME

BUT SOMEHOW THEY WILL FIND A WAY TO EASE THEIR WAY INTO MY REALITY

Oct. 12. 11
L.I.F.E.//

SOMETIMES I WONDER, "IS THIS WHERE I WANT TO BE?" I KNOW EVERYTHING IN LIFE WE DO NOW PREPARES US FOR THE ROAD AHEAD. EVERY MISTAKE I MADE IN THE PAST, I APPRECIATE IT. THE REASON IS I KNOW WHERE I FALL SHORT AT AND I KNOW WHAT STEPPING STONES TO STEP ON. LIFE; LESSONS INSTILLED FOR EVER

2011 09 December
WILL YOU?

Will you let me introduce you to my world for one night
Lay you on the bed and discover those tender spots across your body
Strip you from your clothes and embrace your skin with my tongue
I want to dig deep in your sea and ride the waves if the mood is right
Feel the rush against my fingers as you prepare to let go all of your orgasmic
Excitement
Will you let me give your inner thighs gentle kisses as you continue to drip
Sweet liquids
Will you let me take your heart captive and show your body what real love is

I HATE YOU

I hate that you use to have those eyes
The ones that saw through my shyness
And saw beauty that I refused to see
I hate that smell that lingered on me
Even after I left you
I hate that my heart started to take over my mind
And controlled my hands to walk downtown, and smile
I hate that I missed you & still do
I refuse to let my emotions show, because it makes me look so weak
But I stopped fighting and accepted my defeat
I hate that my body throbs every day for that infectious touch
And it just won't stop

Jan.17, 2012

How

How does it feel to be rescued
To disappear from it all
How does it feel to fall in love
With no one to catch you at the bottom
How do we love at first sight
When our hearts are blind
Why do I seem to want you
When you was never mines

Jan. 12. 2012

Road Map

I want to seek your heart
Because you tend to hide
I wonder what you think at night
When I'm not by your side
Do you kiss with your eyes close
Or do you leave one slightly open
If so, I want to enter your soul
Through the entry of it all
When you are ready to pursue
The reality of your dreams
Come open your heart and let it guide
Its way to me

Jan. 9, 2012

Raindrops

The raindrops that pours from the depths of her soul

Pulled from those experiences that she forced to forget

And it somehow found its way back to her memory

Scared to show the world that side; those stormy nights

That occurred in her life

So the best way she could, she kept those secrets in a sealed bottled

A smile is only a painted sunshine of what they want to see

But underneath is a deserted canvas with a paintbrush no where in sight

When you pull back the mask she hides behind

Her heart cries aloud; seeking love

Jan. 5. 2012

Butterfly Effect

A cocoon is a cocoon

And gradually it matures

And goes through

A process

Of finding its identity

Preparing for what the

World is not ready

To accept

And when

That cocoon is ready to reveal

Who it truly is on the inside

It will be beautiful

True beauty

Starts from the inside

Jan. 30. 2012

I Saw

I saw you

You were walking across the intersection

Midway between my heart and a heartache

On broken boulevard

I decided to meet you halfway and you failed to follow the signs

When we came to a green light, you decided to stop

And when I looked beside me, you was no where by my side

Jan. 17, 2012
Let Me Know

Let me know is it real
You know
From our first kiss
The first moment you captured my eye
Let me know
Is this how love is supposed to feel
Because I never quite had someone like you
That chose to look past the physicality
To get to know me emotionally
But if you are not here to stay long
Save me the trouble and
Let me know

Jan. 12, 2012
Getting Over

The worse feeling is when it finally hits that you cannot have what is not yours. No matter how hard you try to discontinue those thoughts and feelings, it tends to find its way back. Lying and telling yourself that you can forget all about it becomes the norm, despite how useless it is.

Roses

Crimson roses
Slightly crisped by the sunlight
That licks the tips of the petals
So close but so far
She is the rejuvenation of life
The reason I wanted to live, she gave me life
Roses are so perfect from the inside out
But we never know the process it takes to become what it is now

Jan. 5, 2012

…..

Today the Sun awoke

And the Birds chirped

Tonight, the moon shined

And the stars glistened

The ocean waved

And the wind danced

Like new-found

Freedom

December 29, 2011
Journey

Her flaws, I saw as beauty

Her pain , I saw it as her being a survivor

It's amazing how close you can be to someone

Grasping on to each moment

And before you can fully treasure the memories

It's all gone

Dec. 31, 2011
Doing it Wrong

Lost in translation of what things are supposed to be

Expectations never amount to what you expect; reality

When good things go bad, just have to remember it's a part of a lesson

Fighting yourself, trying to deal and accept what has become

And if you tend to lose what you care most about

All you can do is fight for it back, or watch it drift away

It's Just life

Nothing good always stay

Dec. 29, 2011
I don't

I don't need to pluck a thousand petals to predict how you feel

I don't have to read my horoscope and see if we fit compatibly

I don't need the blessings of our friends and family

For me to know how special you are to me

Is all I need is for you to understand

Even when the sun is not shining

And the moon is not full

Just look up at the stars

And remember like them, I will always be close to you

Dec. 29, 2011
Dagger

That piercing feeling

The one that you feel when all else fails   The one that tortures your heart

With the flames of Hell   It hurts

Overwhelming emotions   When all you want to do is die

When you can't bear it all   Restless nights

Because you can't deal with the pain   That sleeps by your bed side

So you take that razor   because you just can't deal

And it takes a couple of slits   Before you realize that nightmare is real

If I

Dear Inner Beauty,

If I could just see you

I would want nothing else

Just to be in the presence

Of someone who is so brilliant

And outstanding

I feel as if my heart smiles

When You are present

Please come out where ever you are

And I promise I will love you forever

Sincerely,

Broken & shattered self

Dec. 28, 2011
Curiosity killed the cat

She wanted to know just how it feels

To involve herself sexually in a new ordeal

After a couple of drinks, she headed to my place

And before we even got started, I was imagining how she taste

To switch things up, we got started in the kitchen

To spice things up, on her neck I started biting and licking

She unbuttoned her shirt , and pulled me close

In less than five minutes I had her out of her clothes

Had her bent over on the counter, biting the inside of her thighs

If eyes could talk, hers would surely be screaming out loud

That night I proved the statement to be a fact

Curiosity did kill the fucking cat

Dec. 28, 2011

If I Fall

I want to fall in a sea of dreams

So when I wake up I can almost believe

In second chances

That maybe the moon will forever

Stay young

And I never

Have to grow old without you

Dec.27, 2011

I rest

My heart in my hands, and bury it in the grave

I lay my life on the boulders that lay next to the sea

Cause when I need you the most

You were nowhere to be found

I fell hard just to find myself in emotional turmoil

Laid at the ground of it all

I fret no more, I learned to do without you

You made me who I am now, someone true

to themselves

So here is my sarcastic thanks to you

For being no fucking help

Dec. 26, 2011

Her

Eyes were like sandpaper

Her touch was inevitable

Her love, untouchable

I saw her in the crowd, alone

Walking with her hair in the wind

And her pride, she wore in her walk

Though I was a just a number in the huge

Crowd

I wanted her to notice me, I wanted to approach her

Until I saw him; he grabbed her by her frail hands and embraced her lips

For a moment, I envision myself in the place of him

Feb. 22. 2012

God knows, I'm not perfect
I'm far from it
It seems so hard to walk down a path
When your eyes are blinded
It is so hard to love
When your heart is broken
All a person can do is try
To be the best that they can be
And if that is not enough
I will always have "me"

March 1, 2012
Chere' Lune,

This morning I tried to grasp onto that little piece of sunlight

The sun turned its back on me, insinuating I would never amount to a star as such as he

So tonight I will continue my journey with the world on my shoulders and as the stars as my guide to a world anew

I will make my way to the moon and ask him to take me under his protection and let me hide

For this world is no place for me, nowhere to reside

The moon slowly replied, you are a greater being than you give credit to yourself to be

Taking shelter behind me will not do you justice

You are a star on the inside, trying to hide away from the world when you are such a sight to see

You see we all have a bit of "moon" mentality

When we find that the time is right, we will eventually shine for the world to see

March 5, 2012
Time

I have so much to say

So little time

With every pace of my heart

That has begun to finally become at ease

No more quickening steps of my heart

As it pace back & forth as it please

Time has passed me by & my heart has finally came to a cease

March 6, 2012

Warmth

That little warmth that a child has as they bury themselves in their blankie

That Sunday morning beam of sun, once the morning dew sets in

A freed mind, no longer held behind boundaries

That small feeling that your crush just might like you

That tingling feeling of returning love back to its rightful owner

All provides a little hope for me on the inside

until I had to realize that the blind-fold was on the whole time

I only dreamed of perfect days and afternoon strolls

Because I had no one to hold on to

Especially when nights like these were cold

Creating childhood scenarios of a promising tomorrow

All were enough to give me temporary warmth

Of something so close enough, but not enough to touch

March 11, 2012

Winters

It was like everything that ever existed

Was obliterated by what has come down to this

Quickening pace of her heart

As they kissed

Winter wonderland

It was like running with wolves

Taking risks with nothing to lose

That's how things use to be

Frost-bitten love

And endless escapades was all they had to remember

Their love was seasonal, they come & go like Cold Winters

March 11, 2012

Walls

She was delicate as a rose that had morning dew on its petals

Yet, she stood strong like walls that stood in corners and places

No one could ever dare stand by

If walls could speak, she would be my personification

She would hold me up when I simply could not find the strength to stand anymore

She would be my solid plain wall

Cause I would fear a wall with a window, someone just might attempt to steal her

soul

And though eventually walls wear out & crack

Like hurricanes tattoo their names to her back

But I knew that from the beginning No one comes equipped with life's tools

And in the end, like the walls, she continued to still be standing too

March 11, 2012

Before you walk away

Give me the chance to show you that there is no one better than me

No one will be able to know why your smile is only a reflection of the wonderful gift

God gave to this world

This earth is so evil & dark

But somehow when I wake up, my world seems to still shine

And you know why?

Because you were next to me

Just the thought of you being mines forever

Is like giving life to a corpse

Giving hope to a empty vase

And if you walk away

Just make sure I'm walking with you

March 12, 2012
Smile

Smile for me even when it hurts you the most

Smile just because you have no clue who treasure your love so closely

Seeing you from a distance eliminates my pain, but feeling you

Hearing you say those words, "I love you" makes my heart go insane

Though you will never know how forcing myself

To thrive off of dead memories

That will no longer become reality

Smile for me, when the thought of me comes across your mind

Smile just to let me know you're happy

Because even when you move on

I want to tell myself that I left a piece of me

Within your memories

March 13, 2012
I realized

I realized that life is full of regrets

gambles, bets and letdowns

It's up to you to either keep up

with life or let it bring you down

Forget the ones who decided to leave

Because they seem to find a way back in your life when you succeed

Don't expect much

And never fall in love

Never fall in love with a touch

Eventually a touch won't be enough

I realized, life seemed to turn around

When i started not to give a fuck

March 19, 2012

Sweet Moments

We argue
We fight

We remain silent
She smiles

She says, "I love it when you're mad"
I sulk

She pushes me down on the bed
We fuck

She bites and sucks on me
I reverse her and lay it on her body

She moans
I listen

Her pussy begins to tighten
She tries to push me off

My fingers are soaking
By her bodily secretions

We argue
We fight

But by the end of the night
We've made sweet moments

March 19, 2012

Your Love

Your love is not possibly possible to explain
It's like trying to find the pieces to a directionless game
It's like falling in love without defining it
Mutually we connect and everything seems so right
But is it fair I call it love, when we're walking in it blinded
Friends we are and forever we will be
My love for you will remain always and because of you
My heart will constantly skip a beat

March 19, 2012
I hate It

I hate it
Trying to recollect preferable memories
That leaves me with such effortless feelings

Wondering & Pondering

If a touch like that will ever be replaced
Not wanting another soul to be offered the opportunity
Only you can access those orgasmic pleasures
Rearrange my mind

To recreate letters into words
That can capture my emotions
Of one night wild escapades
Not like a typical lady, single sentence
But more like a flawless paragraph
With endless words in a world of experiences

February 8, 2012

Screaming Pain
Torturing soul
Broken glass
No longer able to hold
What's inside
Lost the key
To the soul of the eye
Whereever you are
Dear God,
Save me
From this
Misery

February 27, 2012

Feel

What do you feel when you wake up to a bright-filled sky
Do you realize
That I'm not by your side
A bridge that connects two broken pieces
A love that is authentically real
Does your heart speed up at the thought of me, I wonder
I'll do anything just to see how it
Feel

Feb. 27, 2012

G.P.S.

Guide my heart in the direction of hope
Because there just might be enough time
For my heart to come to amends and grow
Discover where the center of true happiness is
Take me down the right path
Because I can't afford any mistakes if you're wrong

March 11, 2012

Goodbyes

Goodbyes are like silent kisses
That take your breath away
As if it can single-handedly annihilate
Everything that mattered yesterday

Like tomorrow is no longer important
Because that last word seemed
To cancel out what life ever meant
To be

Goodbyes are killers of the weakened heart
To see the one you care for
Slowly distant themselves apart
As if happiness never existed
Because when they walk away
It's like you almost could breathe
But missed it

It's like seeing someone with your heart walk away
Because you couldn't find the words to say
So you put on an armour of defeat
Assuming that it just might be easy

For when the moment finally arrives

Don't be surprised if I don't cry
Please believe me, I'll try
It's not that I don't care
Or too strong not to shed a tear
It's just my shallow heart refuses to try

For we both know that day will come
When you finally say, "Goodbye"

www.ingramcontent.com/pod-product-compliance
Ingram Content Group UK Ltd.
Pitfield, Milton Keynes, MK11 3LW, UK
UKHW051134260726
13967UKWH00010B/3034

9 781105 610127